THIS BOOK BELONGS TO

....

Given by

....

Date

....

Special Message

....

....

....

And I [John] saw...them that had gotten the victory over the beast, and over his image, and over his mark, and over the number of his name...saying:

Great and marvellous are thy works,
Lord God Almighty;
just and true are thy ways,
thou King of saints.
Who shall not fear thee, O Lord,
and glorify thy name?
for thou only art holy:
for all nations shall come
and worship before thee;
for thy judgments are made manifest.

Revelation 15:2-4

I Won't Take the Mark
Copyright ©2014 by Katherine Albrecht, EdD
ISBN 978-0-9882802-1-2

VIRTUE PRESS

Published by Virtue Press
A division of Albrecht Media, LLC
www.VirtuePress.com
Orders: 1-855-MarkBook
(1-855-627-5266)

Scripture is quoted from the King James Version of the Holy Bible.

Salvation prayer inspired by Robin Khoury, Executive Director,
Little Light Ministries and Christian School, www.SalvationKids.com.

Illustrations by Julia Pearson.
Illustrations derived from various artists including Lars Justinen,
Greg Olsen and Pat Marvenko Smith.
Patterns and borders © AlfredoM Graphic Arts Studio, *www.alfredom.com*.
Cover and interior design by Monica Thomas for TLC Graphics, *www.TLCGraphics.com*.

Printed and bound in Canada.

I Won't Take the Mark

A Bible Book and Contract for Children

by Katherine Albrecht, EdD

Nurtured by Tiffany Daschke & Katina Michael, PhD

VIRTUE PRESS ~ www.VirtuePress.com

Dedicated to the memory of

my wise and witty grandmother

Evalyn Muriel Woodall,

my generous and resourceful mother Elaine,

and the millions of parents

and grandparents who have passed

this knowledge down through

the generations.

Dr. Katherine Albrecht

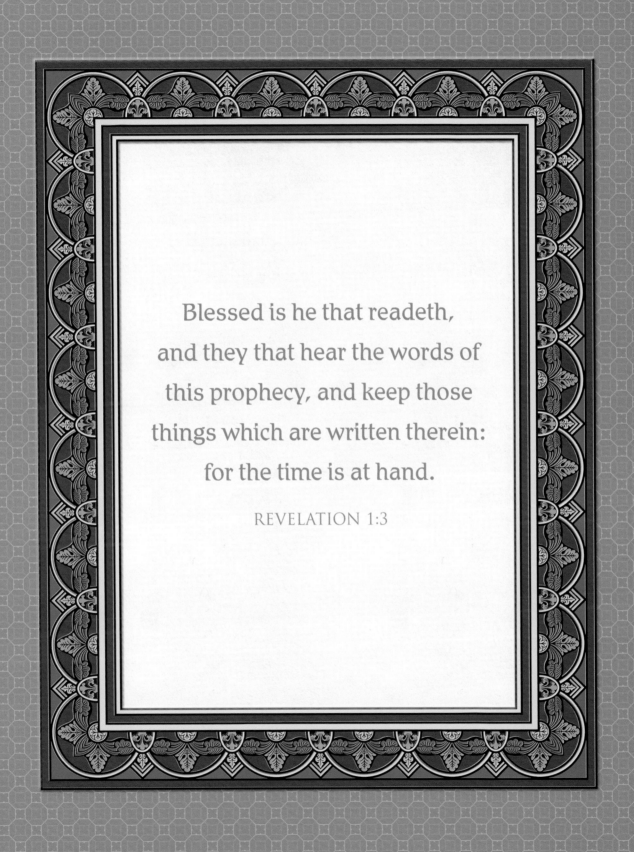

Blessed is he that readeth,
and they that hear the words of
this prophecy, and keep those
things which are written therein:
for the time is at hand.

REVELATION 1:3

When Jesus lived long ago, things were much simpler.

There were no televisions or computers. There were no cell phones or credit cards.

People bought things with coins made of silver, bronze, and gold.

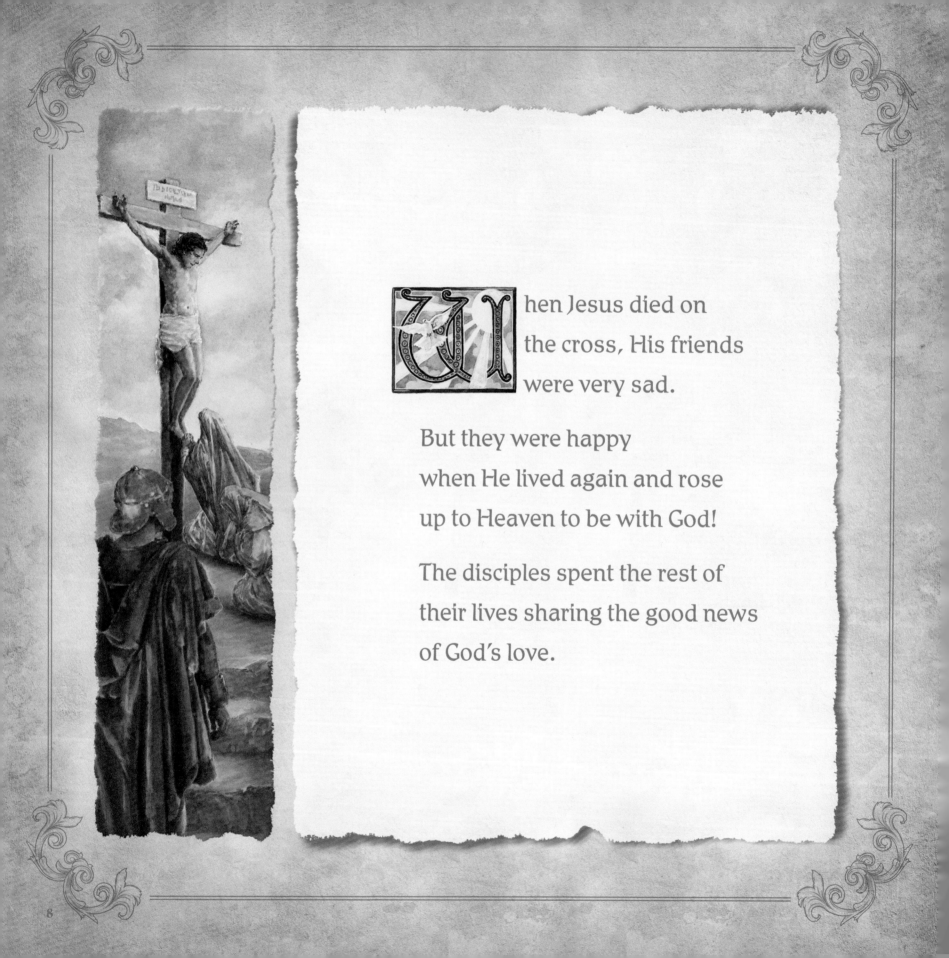

When Jesus died on the cross, His friends were very sad.

But they were happy when He lived again and rose up to Heaven to be with God!

The disciples spent the rest of their lives sharing the good news of God's love.

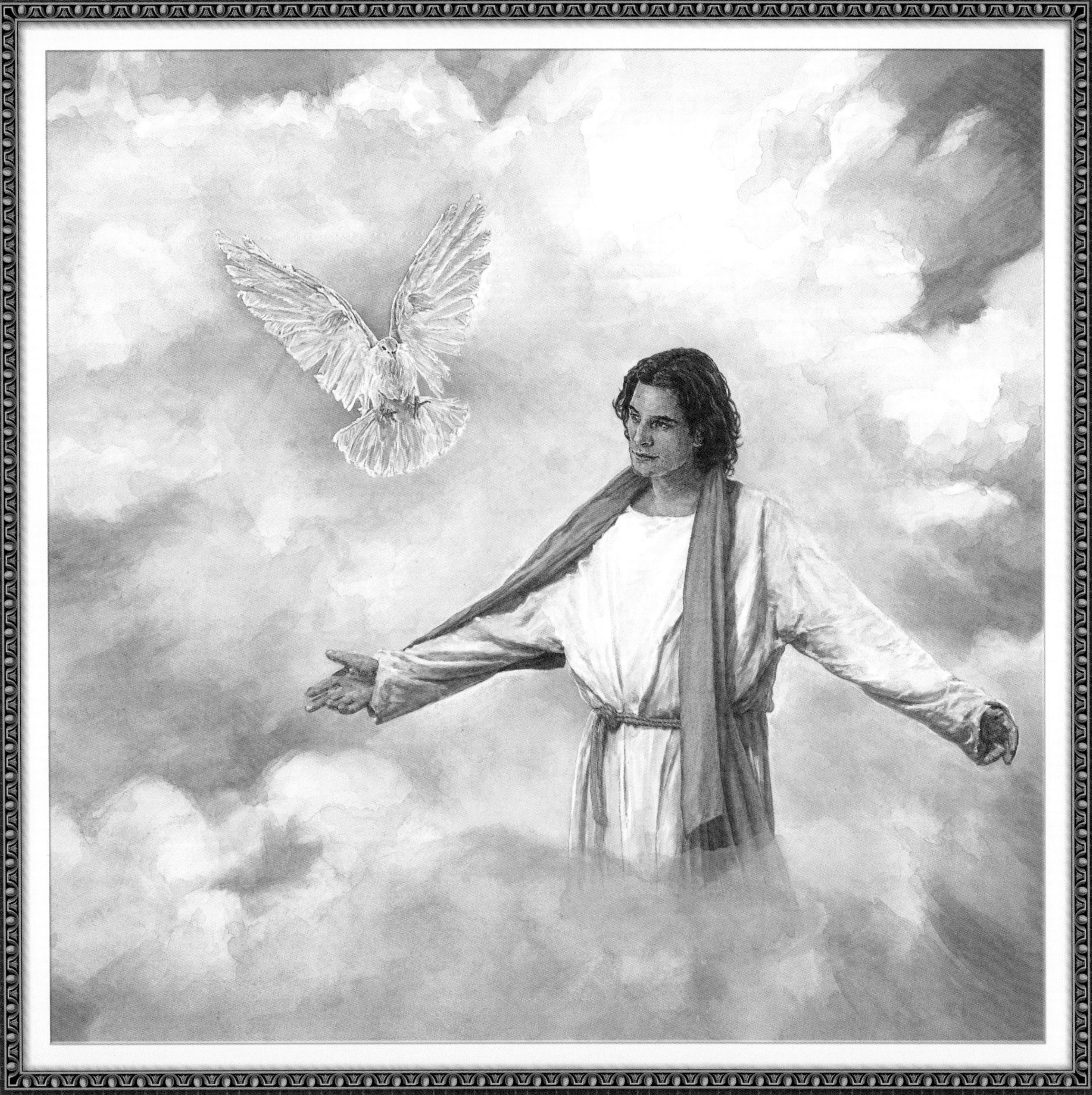

One of the disciples was named John.

When John was an old man, he saw an amazing vision.

Jesus took him to Heaven to see the future. John saw many ways the world would change.

John saw that one day a bad leader will rule the whole world. The Bible calls him the beast.

He may seem like a wonderful man, but he will be mean and cruel. He will hate God and His people.

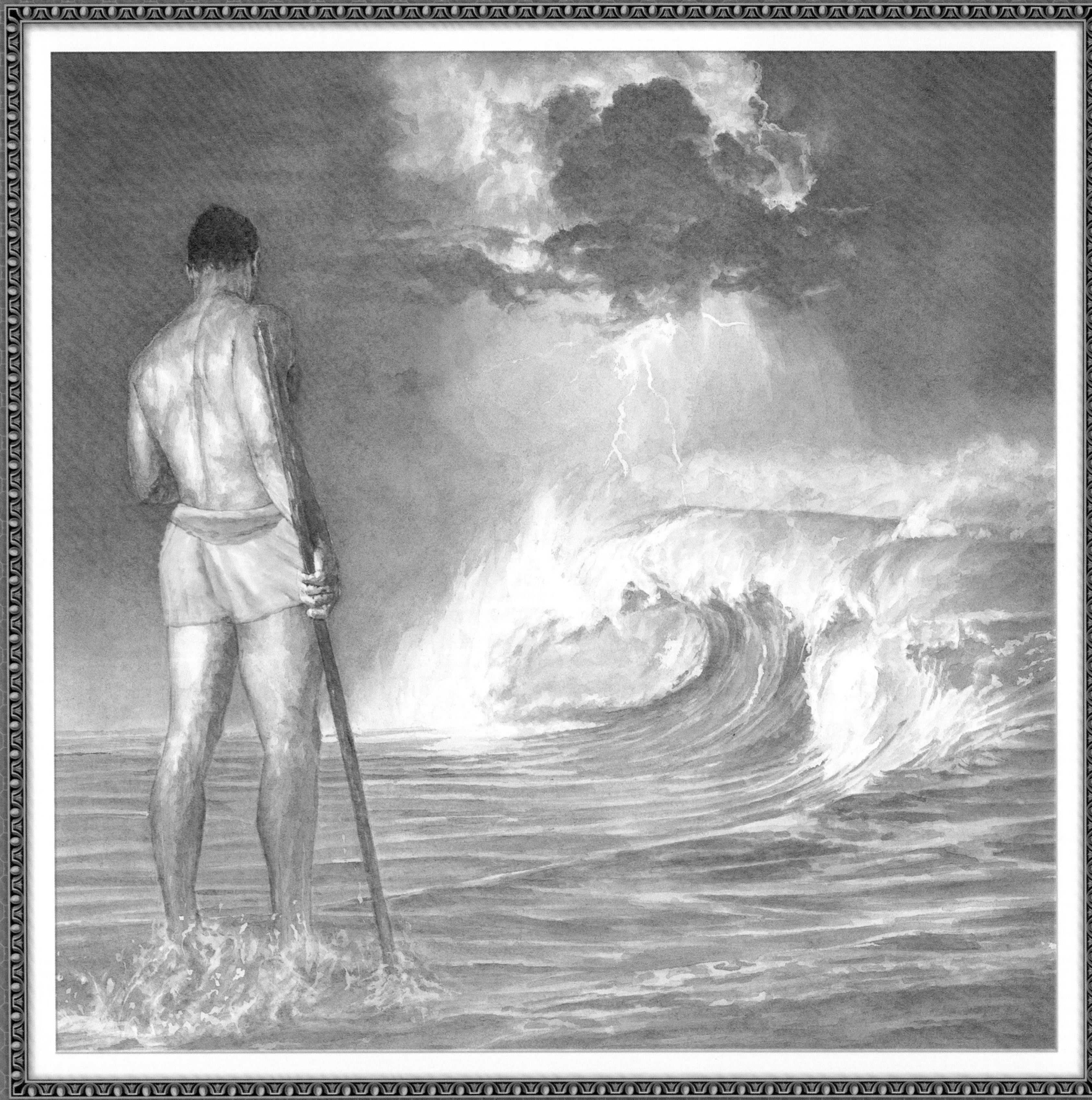

The beast will act like he is God, but he will get his power from the devil.

He will fool many people and get them to obey him and worship him.

The beast will try to put a mark on every person in the world.

Each mark will have a name or a number in it. The number will be 666.

We don't know what the mark will look like, but God's people will recognize it when it comes.

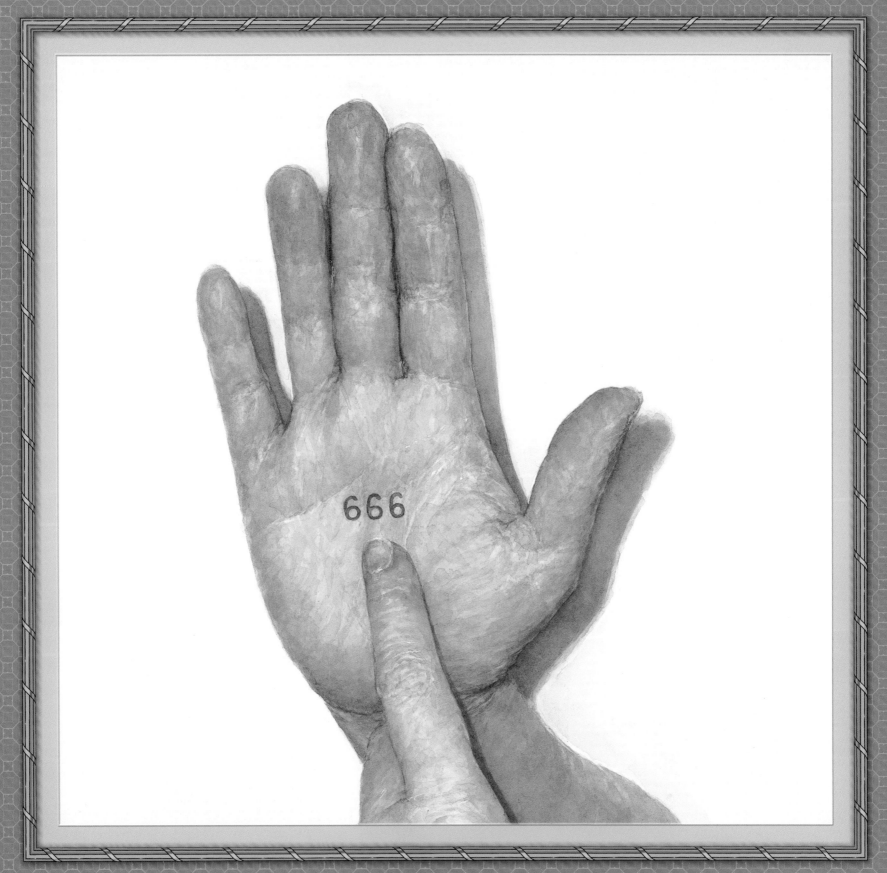

And that no man might buy or sell, save he that had the mark, or the name of the beast, or the number of his name.

REVELATION 13:17

People will be forced to worship the beast and take his mark in their right hand or their forehead.

If they don't have the mark, they won't be able to buy or sell.

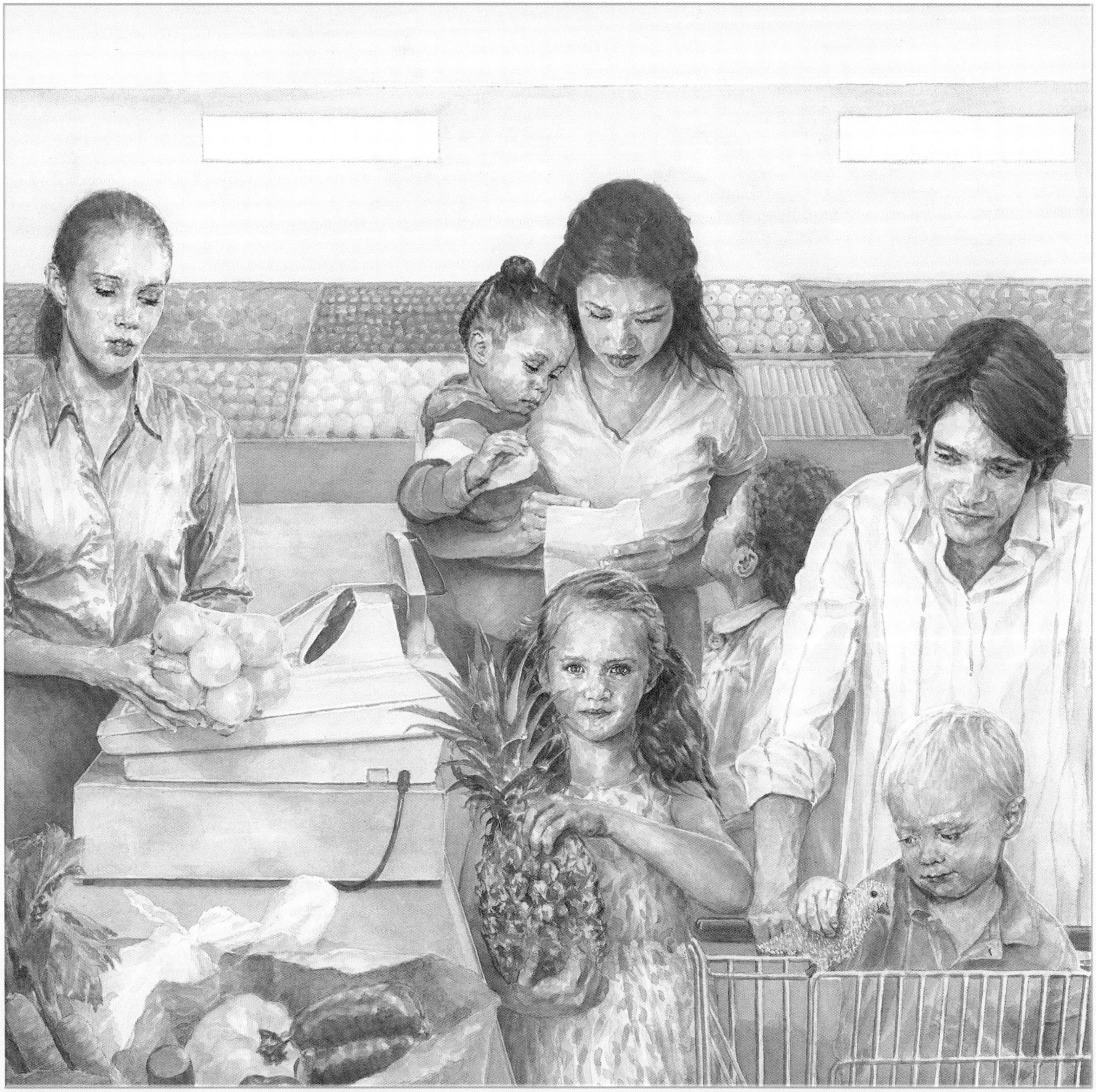

(And an angel said) *with a loud voice, If any man worship the beast and his image, and receive [his] mark in his forehead, or in his hand,*

The same shall drink of the wine of the wrath of God, which is poured out without mixture into the cup of his indignation; and he shall be tormented with fire and brimstone in the presence of the holy angels, and in the presence of the Lamb:

And the smoke of their torment ascendeth up for ever and ever: and they have no rest day nor night, who worship the beast and his image, and whosoever receiveth the mark of his name.

REVELATION 14:9–11

ut God's people will say No. They will never take the mark, because they know it is bad.

God will punish the people who worship the beast and take his mark.

And it was given unto him to make war with the saints, and to overcome them...
REVELATION 13:7

And he had power to...cause that as many as would not worship the image of the beast should be killed.
REVELATION 13:15

...I [saw] the souls of them that were beheaded for the witness of Jesus, and for the word of God, and which had not worshipped the beast, neither his image, neither had received his mark upon their foreheads, or in their hands...
REVELATION 20:4

Here is the patience of the saints: here [are] they that keep the commandments of God, and the faith of Jesus.

And I heard a voice from heaven saying unto me, Write, Blessed [are] the dead which die in the Lord from henceforth: Yea, saith the Spirit, that they may rest from their labours; and their works do follow them.
REVELATION 14:12-13

...I saw under the altar the souls of them that were slain for the word of God, and for the testimony which they held:

And they cried with a loud voice, saying, How long, O Lord, holy and true, dost thou not judge and avenge our blood on them that dwell on the earth?

And white robes were given unto every one of them; and it was said unto them, that they should rest yet for a little season, until their fellowservants also and their brethren, that should be killed as they [were], should be fulfilled.
REVELATION 6:9-11

 he beast will be very angry when God's people refuse to get the mark.

He will even kill them.

But don't worry. God will reward His brave and faithful followers.

And a voice came out of the throne, saying, Praise our God, all ye his servants, and ye that fear him, both small and great.

And I heard as it were the voice of a great multitude, and as the voice of many waters, and as the voice of mighty thunderings, saying, Alleluia: for the Lord God omnipotent reigneth.

Let us be glad and rejoice, and give honour to him: for the marriage of the Lamb is come, and his wife hath made herself ready.

And to her was granted that she should be arrayed in fine linen, clean and white: for the fine linen is the righteousness of saints.

And he saith unto me, Write, Blessed [are] they which are called unto the marriage supper of the Lamb...

REVELATION 19:5-9

There will be great rejoicing when God welcomes His faithful people into His kingdom.

Those who did not worship the beast will celebrate!

And the beast was taken, and with him the false prophet that wrought miracles before him, with which he deceived them that had received the mark of the beast, and them that worshipped his image. These both were cast alive into a lake of fire burning with brimstone.

REVELATION 19:20

And I saw an angel come down from heaven, having the key of the bottomless pit and a great chain in his hand. And he laid hold on the dragon, that old serpent, which is the Devil, and Satan, and bound him a thousand years:

And cast him into the bottomless pit, and shut him up, and set a seal upon him, that he should deceive the nations no more, till the thousand years should be fulfilled...

REVELATION 20:1-3

ohn's vision was scary. But it had a great ending!

Jesus will return and fight against the beast and win. Then an angel will throw the devil into a pit and lock him up where he can't hurt people any more.

And I saw thrones, and they sat upon them, and judgment was given unto them: and [I saw] the souls of them that were beheaded for the witness of Jesus, and for the word of God, and which had not worshipped the beast, neither his image, neither had received [his] mark upon their foreheads, or in their hands; and they lived and reigned with Christ a thousand years.

But the rest of the dead lived not again until the thousand years were finished. This [is] the first resurrection.

Blessed and holy [is] he that hath part in the first resurrection: on such the second death hath no power, but they shall be priests of God and of Christ, and shall reign with him a thousand years.

REVELATION 20:4-6

After that, everyone who refused the mark of the beast will get a special reward.

They will have a beautiful new life with Jesus!

They will become his priests and live and reign with him for a thousand years.

And I saw a new heaven and a new earth: for the first heaven and the first earth were passed away; and there was no more sea.

And I John saw the holy city, new Jerusalem, coming down from God out of heaven, prepared as a bride adorned for her husband.

And I heard a great voice out of heaven saying, Behold, the tabernacle of God [is] with men, and he will dwell with them, and they shall be his people, and God himself shall be with them, [and be] their God.

And God shall wipe away all tears from their eyes; and there shall be no more death, neither sorrow, nor crying, neither shall there be any more pain: for the former things are passed away.

REVELATION 21:1-4

od will make a new Heaven and a new Earth where everything is beautiful and good.

His people will live with Him and be happy. They will never be sad again!

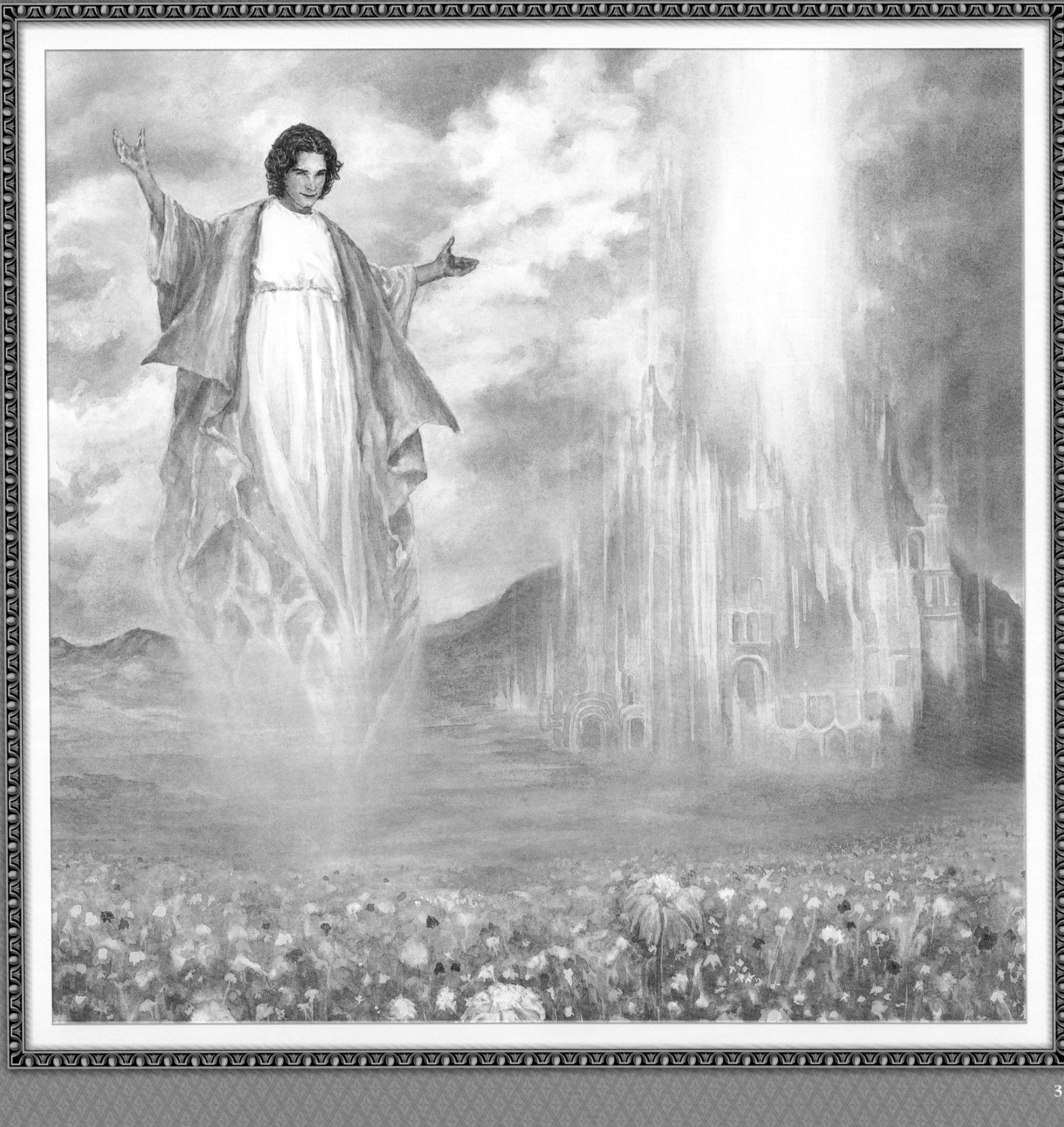

hen John's vision was over, Jesus told him to write down everything he had seen.

John wrote it in a book called Revelation. Revelation is the last book in the Bible.

Revelation was hard for people to understand.

They did not know how a mark or a number could be used to buy and sell.

Today people pay with numbers when they use a credit card, wave a payment wristband, or swipe their phone. Some people have even put computer chips in their hands with numbers inside.

When people get used to these things, they may agree to accept the beast's mark.

s the beast coming? Yes. We know everything the Bible tells us is true.

But we don't know when it will happen. These things may happen soon, or they may not happen for a very long time.

But we do know this: God loves us and He is in control!

Behold, I stand at the door, and knock: if any man hear my voice, and open the door, I will come in to him, and will sup with him, and he with me.

To him that overcometh will I grant to sit with me in my throne, even as I also overcame, and am set down with my Father in his throne.

REVELATION 3:20-21

Let that therefore abide in you, which ye have heard from the beginning. If that which ye have heard from the beginning shall remain in you, ye also shall continue in the Son, and in the Father.

And this is the promise that he hath promised us, [even] eternal life.

1 JOHN 2:24-25

But continue thou in the things which thou hast learned and hast been assured of, knowing of whom thou hast learned [them];

And that from a child thou hast known the holy scriptures, which are able to make thee wise unto salvation through faith which is in Christ Jesus.

2 TIMOTHY 3:14-15

You don't have to be afraid of the beast or his mark.

You can pray for Jesus to come into your life to save you and give you courage. That special prayer is at the end of this book.

God does not want anyone to worship the beast or take his mark. He wants us to belong only to Him.

Will you promise to trust in God and never take the mark of the beast?

(Fill out the certificate now.)

Here is a place where you can record your promise.

I love God and I promise to obey Him.

I will never worship anyone but God,
and I will never take the mark of the beast.

I will call on Jesus Christ to save me and
help me keep my promise.

WRITE YOUR NAME ....

WITNESSED BY ....

DATE ....

A Note to Parents and Grandparents
from Dr. Katherine Albrecht

My grandmother warned me about the mark of the beast when I was a little girl. That conversation in the kitchen of a farmhouse decades ago changed the course of my life.

When I was a child there were no personal computers, no cell phones, no Internet or high speed satellite communications. I had never seen a credit card. The things my mother bought at the store still had real price tags, not bar codes, and she paid in cash—like everyone else. I couldn't imagine a time when every purchase could be made with a number.

Fast forward, and today the words of John's prophesy no longer seem so distant or hard to envision. For the first time in history, the mark of the beast is technologically possible. After two thousand years that scholars have puzzled over how things could be bought and sold with a number, this generation is the first to see that vision become a reality. More shocking still, it is hard to believe we live in a time when a number can be put into a person's body.

You can help your children practice saying "no" to the mark of the beast whenever you visit a museum, carnival, or amusement park. Refuse to wear wristbands with payment chips inside. Tell the staff you have a religious objection to a mark being placed on your child's hand or forehead, so you do not permit your child to receive a hand stamp for re-entry or face painting on the forehead.

While hand stamps and face painting are harmless in their current form, teaching your children to refuse them will set a precedent in their lives and help them practice standing up for their beliefs.

Many Christians (myself included) are also concerned about biometric payment technologies that use the hand, such as fingerprint readers. If you share these concerns, please speak out against their use.

Parents and grandparents are a huge influence on children. A word aptly spoken to a child today is like a seed that may later flourish into understanding and saving faith tomorrow. It did in my case.

Sincerely,
Dr. Katherine Albrecht, EdD
www.KatherineAlbrecht.com

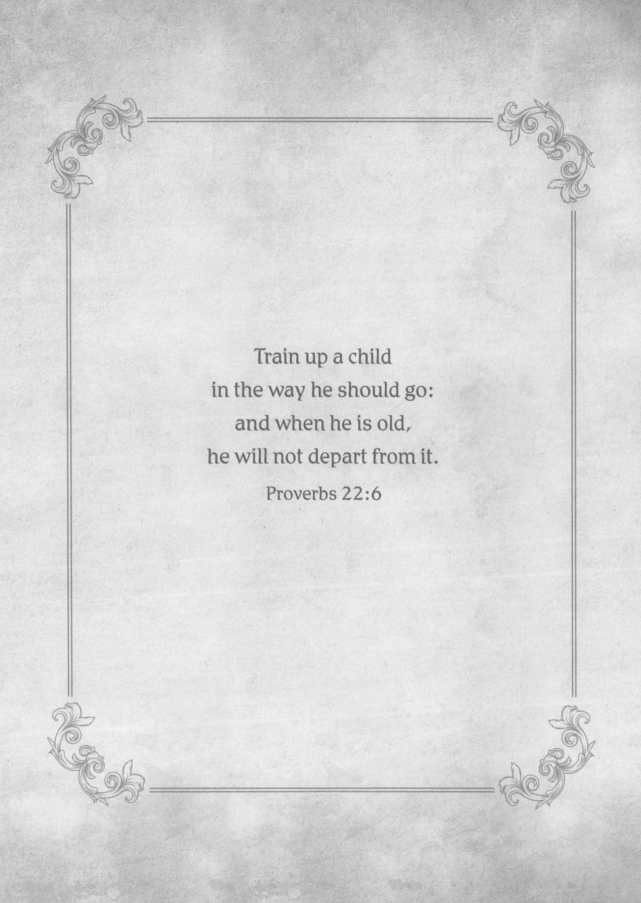

Train up a child
in the way he should go:
and when he is old,
he will not depart from it.

Proverbs 22:6